A CHANGED AMERICA

A brief study of how American life has changed during the last few years

KevyArgy

ISBN 13: 978-93-5530-125-3
ISBN 10: 93-5530-125-1

Published by BUUKS.

Library of Congress Registration Number: TXu 2-278-114
Author e-mail: kevyargy@gmail.com
Author website: kevyargywriter.com

PREFACE

I am dedicating this book to all the people who migrated to America and faced prejudice, discrimination, obstacles and struggled to live the American dream.

Immigrants are of different genres. Some of them come here not by choice, but because they were forced to leave their homes due to political or religious persecution, poverty, corruption, violence, etc. Some come out of their own choice to pursue higher education or in search of better jobs and prospects. Many leave their well-paying jobs behind in search of greener pastures on the other side, but end up ruining their lives because of the clash with the new culture. This cultural conflict reflects in their American born children who think and behave differently than their parents.

The fact is that prejudice and discrimination do not just exist among the natives, immigrants also bring their own baggage of prejudice and discrimination which reflects in their interactions with the natives and among themselves.

Some people come here with a false assumption that their "brown" skin color is "white." They think of themselves as "Whites" as their skin color is considered the same back in their countries not knowing that their skin color is not considered as "white" here.

We may claim that we are as unbiased as we pretend to be, but are we? So, whom can we blame?

The truth is we are living in a dangerous world on the mercy of a few people in powerful positions who can control our lives by taking advantage of our weakness and vulnerability. We are also at the mercy of rapists, murderers, robbers, kidnappers and some mentally ill, anti-social, stupid, disordered egoistic people who think they are superior to others because of their skin color or race and always try to discriminate, dominate, bully and threaten those who are vulnerable and whom they don't like because of their race, religion, cast, and politics. We are also at the mercy of natural calamities and pandemics, and one should be lucky enough to survive all these in their lifetime.

Is there a community in the world which is not biased? Most people like their own kind and show prejudice towards others when they get a chance. But, when they get the same treatment from another community, they play victims and try to get sympathy and justice from the public as if they are helpless, innocent victims.

An immigrant who was a co-worker of mine once told me, "As long as, I get a paycheck every week and pay my bills, I don't care which party wins, which party loses or who governs."

"Moreover, we are here to make a living, so nothing matters. Whether it is discrimination, prejudice, ridicule or anything at all," said another immigrant. He also added, "We did the same thing when a foreigner visited our country. We used to ridicule them in our language for fun. So, I don't care if, I get the same treatment here."

I am not trying to impress the readers as a scholar, historian or a vocabulary expert, and not criticizing politics or politicians or pointing a finger or siding with anything or anyone, but rather trying to convey my observations of the changes, I experienced while living in this country in the last few decades.

People's opinions differ. It doesn't have to be the same as the writer's. It is in the discretion of the readers to choose their own viewpoints.

CHAPTER ONE

During my school and college days, I read several travelogues written by native writers who visited the U.S., I also read many books on American life and culture from the library of "American Cultural Center" which was located in the city where I attended college back in my home country.

In the travelogues, the writers wrote great things about this country and even described it as "the land where milk and honey flows."

They wrote that everyone regardless of their occupation drives a car, owns a home with TV, fridge, AC, phone, etc. which were a luxury in my home country at that time. The streets were so clean as nobody even threw a piece of paper or spit on the streets. People always disposed garbage in the bins kept on the sidewalks. Everyone obeyed the law and the stores that sell items like newspapers, leave their stuff outside, in front of the stores, and nobody stole them.

I always wished to visit this wonderful country one day, and I got that opportunity in 1986 when I landed in New York.

I was a little disappointed after the arrival because some of the impressions and expectations I had from the travelogues I read were not found exactly the way they were supposed to be.

I realized that the real America is not the same as what I read in the travelogues because those writers who visited only for a brief period of time, and that was the impression they got within that time frame.

To know what the real America is, one has to live here for a long enough time and experience it on a day-to-day basis.

I found that not all the streets here were as clean as expected. Maybe they were cleaner at the time when those writers visited. (Of course, they are cleaner than in many other countries.)

Even though people spoke English better than a well-educated person from a foreign country where English is a second language, I was surprised to know that not everyone was educated. Back in my home country if someone spoke good English, they were considered a well-educated person who also held a good position at work and prestige in the society. I could not believe that there are hundreds of people here who are illiterate even though they spoke English more fluently than a well-educated person from a foreign country. But, I noticed a peculiar thing. The old immigrants were keen to show their expertise in English to the new ones even though their English was not understood well by the natives!

While walking on the streets, I hear English more with a foreign accent as the number of immigrants settled in the country has been growing steadily, especially in major cities.

As a young boy, I thought that everyone would be formally dressed, in a suit and tie always, but surprisingly, I found most of the people in casual outfits like jeans and T-shirts. But, I noticed that most of the immigrants were particular in wearing a suit and tie especially for every occasion in their community that they attended!

Also, as funny as it may seem, in my school days, I innocently thought that all the people in America were super rich, and they would be able and willing to give away any amount of money if someone asked for help. But, I found the reality was different than I thought. When I started living here, I noticed that there was a wide gap between the richest, the rich, the middle-class, the lower-middle class and poor. According to a study, the U.S. has the highest inequality among developed countries though it is the wealthiest country in history. Maybe everyone owns a car, but many of them are on loan or lease or used ones which are bought for a cheaper price, and most of the homes which people live in are mortgaged.

I could not believe my eyes when I saw beggars (panhandlers as they are called here) on the streets and on subway trains. On sidewalks of the streets people were sitting with signboards such as "Homeless and unemployed," "Hungry please help," etc., placed in front of them. In trains, people gave small speeches saying that they were unemployed or homeless and needed money to buy food. Some played musical instruments or sang songs and asked for money. And on the subway train platforms people played musical instruments and sang while keeping a small basket or hat in front of them for commuters to drop money. I was wondering whether they were displaying their talents by singing and playing musical instruments to the public or was it another way of panhandling! Whatever the truth is, it is unbelievable that it happens here, the richest country on Earth! I was under the impression that poverty and homelessness existed only in the so called third world countries. I never ever imagined that there could be poverty and homelessness in America, the land of milk and honey as it was described in the travelogues I read, and the one country where everyone around the world dreams to migrate.

Back in my home country, I have seen children and adults flock around foreign tourists, especially from America and European countries, and beg for money as they think that they were all very rich. But, I had never imagined that one day an American would beg money from me. People stopped me on the streets and asked for money to pay for a meal or a cup of coffee, and sometimes even for a mere 25 cents. Later, I came to know that most of these homeless and panhandlers are either alcoholics or drug addicts who have no other income or had lost their means to earn. I also learned that there are millions of people, including children, who are living in poverty because of alcoholism and drug addiction besides divorce.

On a visit to Los Angeles, I saw a whole street in downtown called 'Skid Row' where people who become homeless for different reasons live. They included drug addicts, mentally ill persons, drug peddlers and criminals who come out of prison after serving their term or on parole and also those who lost their job, income and everything. For all these people, 'Skid Row' is their home and also a place where drugs are easily available as it is a haven for drug dealers too.

I also observed that the majority of the people living in the cities are not all White Americans as I thought. A few years back, there were 89% White Americans in large cities, but now it is less than 69%. Most of them moved out to suburban areas, as the immigrants who come from different countries around the world started settling in these cities. The same way, they moved out when Blacks moved into bigger homes in White neighborhoods in the 50's and 60's.

CHAPTER TWO

After the terrorist attacks on September 11, 2001, the mentality of people towards Muslims or those perceived to be Muslims, including South Asian descent especially 'Sikhs' (Indians with turban and beard), changed dramatically.

People were gripped with fear and paranoia. Several people who fitted a certain description were attacked or killed in hate. Immediately after the attacks, a Sikh businessman originally from India was mistaken for a Muslim and murdered. In schools, Muslim and several South Asian children were ridiculed and called names such as 'Osama' 'Bin Laden,' etc.

Hostility and hate crimes against Muslims and other immigrants increased and hundreds of hate crimes were reported in the following years after 9/11.

Most people hold a pre-judgmental and stereotypical presumption about others and cannot differentiate the origin of a person from one to another. Because of my physical features such as mustache, brown skin color etc., I started to become nervous out of fear about how people might perceive me. To make things worse, I was chosen for additional security screenings at airports whenever I took flights, maybe because of my looks and the foreign sounding last name.

Once, I was returning from my home country after a vacation. I was chosen for additional questioning by immigration officials even though, I had an American passport, maybe because they could not accept me as an American citizen. I was detained and asked to narrate the procedure for becoming an American citizen through naturalization as if I was an imposter.

I was under the impression that holding an American passport would be more credible than having a green card. But to my dismay it did not make any difference for the immigration officials whether I am a green card holder or an American citizen as long as I looked like a foreigner.

Luckily, after the questioning and checking my background, they let me go as they found me clean. But it felt like a nightmare. I was wondering what if they have detained me without letting me go and if they did so, how long would it have taken before I got freed? This incident made me more nervous especially when traveling by air.

There were several incidents where passengers were asked to vacate the aircrafts just because other passengers expressed concern about traveling with them because they were sporting a mustache or beard.

'Islamophobia' became a pervasive feature of American public life.

In 2015, a 14-year-old schoolboy who happened to be a Muslim was arrested by police in Texas because he brought a digital clock made by him to the school for his engineering project. The school authorities got suspicious, and they informed the police. He was later released, but his parents and their relatives were left in a great shock. To their surprise, President Obama congratulated him for his invention and even invited him to the White House. Later the boy and his parents decided to go back to their country of origin in the Middle East to continue his education so that they could escape the 'Islamophobia' which has been growing among people in this country.

A couple of famous Indian movie stars who came for a visit were detained for questioning in New York and New Jersey airports by immigration officials just because they had Muslim names.

In another incident, a group of actors also from India, while flying in a domestic flight to perform in a cultural stage show in New York were mistaken for terrorists because they were speaking a foreign language, and also some of their gestures which they were exchanging as the rehearsal for their acts in the show made some passengers nervous and suspicious of them and informed the crew. The crew then informed the Homeland Security Department, and two military planes were deployed immediately to escort the flight until they reached LaGuardia airport where the flight was heading. The group was detained when the flight landed and whisked away for questioning. The questioning continued for hours until the organizers of the show who were waiting at the airport to receive them approached the officials, and the Indian Consulate convinced them with an explanation.

One day, a woman overheard a conversation of a group of foreign youngsters in their language in a restaurant and thought that she heard words like 'bomb' and 'explosives' which might have been misunderstood by her because of the foreign language they spoke, and she decided to call the police. The police came and kept vigilance on them and followed their car when they left the restaurant for several miles, only to find out that they were students who were going to join a college. All of this at the expense of government's thousands of dollars!

One day, I decided to shave off my mustache thinking that it might help to get rid of my stereotypical look and ease my nervousness and anxiety in public places as I used to become nervous when people looked or stared at me. But unfortunately, shaving off the mustache did not seem to be of much help as I got the same treatment at airports and other places and situations because I looked the same stereotypical foreigner who is only clean shaven!

It reminded me of the story about a Black person who tried to peel off his skin to get rid of the frustration for having black skin color during the slavery era.

I would like to emphasize that these are my personal feelings and experiences only and not necessarily that others who have similar looks and features as mine would have experienced or felt the same.

In fact, some of my friends who are also immigrants claimed that they didn't feel the same as I felt. But, I am not sure whether they were telling the truth or not. Maybe, I am more sensitive than them, or they have a thicker skin than I do. Whatever it is, the immigrants are labelled as 'Resident Alien' on the green cards for a reason – an outsider living in the country.

Every immigrant would have faced some kind of discrimination sometime in their life for sure. If anyone says 'no,' either they are lying or are living in denial.

Maybe, most of them do not reveal to avoid embarrassment or pretend that there is no problem at all.

In 2015, an old Indian man was taking a walk in the neighborhood of his son's home in Huntsville, Alabama where he was living while on a visit. Someone noticed him looking into the garages of homes inquisitively and called the police to report a 'suspicious' looking foreigner walking around the neighborhood. Police came and stopped him for questioning, but he was unable to understand and answer them clearly as he was not proficient with American English. And, he kept putting his hands nervously in his pants' pockets, and police suspected that he might be reaching for a weapon and so the cops tried to pat him. As he was unfamiliar with the procedure, he tried to pull away. That provoked the cops, and they forced him down on the ground and tried to hand cuff him. In the melee, the man got injured and partially paralyzed, and he had to be admitted into a hospital. He underwent surgery, but did not recover fully. Didn't this happen because of his looks and skin color?

After 9/11, security measures were enforced very strictly across public places such as train stations, bus terminals, airports, etc. It became a common sigh to see police dogs in most of these public places, and the dogs were trained to sniff bags, briefcases and other luggage which are carried by the people to detect weapons, bombs or any other explosives.

Once someone was caught at an airport with a bomb fitted inside the sole of his shoes. He became known as "the shoe bomber." This was followed by a rule to remove shoes of all the passengers and screen before boarding the planes.

This was followed by another man who got caught with a bottle of some sports drink which contained explosives, and all of a sudden, another rule came into effect that passengers should not be allowed to carry any kind of liquid, even drinking water, beyond the security screening area.

And very soon x-ray scanners were installed at most of the leading airports to get a full body scan of the passengers. Even though most of the passengers, especially women, were uncomfortable with this idea, they had no choice but to oblige along with many other rules which were really inconvenient to the passengers.

In June 2018, any kind of powder-like substances were banned inside the cabin baggage or handbags after a foiled attempt to use 'powder-like explosives' on a flight to the U.S. from Australia.

It came to a point that people didn't feel safe to travel. They were wondering what could come next?

In the meantime, a shocking trend of homegrown terrorists who were sympathizers to the terrorist groups started blossoming in the country. Most of them were U.S. born youngsters, including non-Muslims who were converting to Islam and getting radicalized to become 'Jihadists.' They even went to Muslim countries to become trained terrorists.

A young man who happened to be a non-Muslim but had converted to Islam was arrested for making bombs. It became a real challenge for the law enforcement officers as they did not know whom to suspect and whom not to, and the home grown sympathizers did not look like the stereotypical terrorists.

In 2015, a U.S. born citizen of Pakistani parents and his fiancée from Saudi Arabia, shot and killed 14 people and injured 22 others at a government social service center's office party hosted in San Bernardino, California. The shooter was also an employee at the service center. Investigators revealed that it was an act of terrorism, and it was also reported that the man had an argument with a co-worker on his religion a few days earlier.

It was also reported that the couple was planning the attack for some time and were collecting ammunition in their apartment where they were living. Despite living in, a residential area, surprisingly even their neighbors didn't suspect anything.

In another incident, a man shot and killed 4 people and injured 53 at a nightclub in Florida. It was also a terrorist act by a radicalized young Muslim, also a U.S. born citizen.

All these homegrown terrorist acts added fuel to the already flaming fire of hate towards Muslims and immigrants.

Some of these incidents included Muslim children getting bullied in schools or facing violence. Once three Muslim boys were shot dead by their neighbor. Mosques and Islamic centers were vandalized and death threats were left on voice mail.

A flight attendant refused to give an unopened soda can to a hijab clad Muslim woman passenger citing security reasons that it could be used as a weapon. A pilot of an airline refused to fly with a couple of Muslim and Sikh passengers. They were asked to leave the plane.

In a major city, a few hijab-clad women were harassed, ridiculed with hateful slurs. They were labelled terrorists, and even attempts were made to rip off their hijabs. A man was kicked off from a flight because he spoke in Arabic on the phone. A 'Sikh' man was not allowed to board a plane because he refused to take off his turban.

Even Hindus and Buddhists were not spared. Hindu temples were vandalized and a Buddhist in a robe was mistaken for a Muslim and assaulted.

In a bar in Kansas, a man of Indian origin was shot dead, and another Indian man critically injured by a person who thought that they were from the Middle East. He shouted "get out of my country" while shooting them.

The "Sikh" people who are originally from India are always mistaken for Muslims. They are the third-most targeted religious group for hate crimes after Jews and Muslims, according to a report. They were ridiculed with calls of 'Bin Laden' or 'Osama' and were attacked and even shot dead at several places in the country. Their temples were vandalized and were targeted with hateful graffiti's, including the word 'ISIS.'

It was difficult to accept that all these incidents were happening in America, the country which stood for "liberty and justice for all."

CHAPTER THREE

On January 20, 2009, Barack Obama was sworn in as the 44th President of the United States.

As, I was watching the inauguration on TV, I noticed tears of joy rolling down from the eyes of Oprah Winfrey and Rev. Jesse Jackson, the greatest supporters of Obama among the cheerful and tearful crowd of more than 18 million people gathered at the Capitol all the way up to the Washington monument to witness that historic moment of Obama taking the Oath.

In his speech he said, "For we, the people, understand that our country cannot succeed when a shrinking few do very well, and a growing many barely make it. We believe that America's prosperity must rest upon the broad shoulders of a rising middle class. We know that America thrives when every person can find independence and pride in their work, when the wages of honest labor liberate families from the brink of hardship. We are true to our creed when a little girl born into the bleakest poverty knows that she has the same chance to succeed as anybody else, because she is an American. She is free and she is equal, not just in the eyes of God, but also in our own."

"We, the people, still believe that every citizen deserves a basic measure of security and dignity. We must make the hard choices to reduce the cost of healthcare and the size of our deficit. But we reject the belief that America must choose between caring for the generation that built this country and investing in the generation that build its future. Our journey is not complete until all our children from the streets of Detroit to the hills of Appalachia to the quiet lanes of Newtown know that they are cared for and cherished and always safe from harm."

He concluded, "Let each of us, embrace with solemn duty and awesome joy what is our lasting birth right. With common effort and common purpose, with passion and dedication, let us answer the call of history and carry into an uncertain future that precious light of freedom."

I was wondering at that time why it took so long for a person who is Black to become the President, even though they were in this country for more than 400 years. Maybe, it was destined for one person, Barack Obama.

Millions of Americans who went to vote on November 4, 2008 would have never believed a Black person could be elected President of the United States of America. Obama won 53% of the popular votes including from Virginia and Indiana where no Democrats had won for a long time. Besides the Black Community who gave him the majority vote, a large demographic group including the blue-collar whites who were ready to support a Black candidate. A lot of youngsters who had never voted before turned out in large numbers to vote, and they voted for Obama. People saw him as a competent, confident leader who represents the aspirations of America. One day people may look back on this Presidential election and wonder how this happened. As many decades ago, especially in the slavery era no one could have ever imagine that a Black person would become President and live in the White House.

His words during the campaign were, "America can change. That is the true genius of this nation." The enthusiasm he generated translated into votes. Also, three years before the election, the disastrous impact of 'Hurricane Katrina' wrecked many Black lives and the government's response betrayed its own racial and class interests, having left Blacks and other poor people so obviously helpless.

The 2008 Presidential contest was history. A female candidate and a Black candidate fighting a war of attention around the country. The issue of race came up, but Obama stayed above the fray.

More than 240,000 people gathered at Grant Park of Chicago's waterfront to mark the historic victory. Obama said to the audience "The road will be steep. We may not get there in one year or even one term. But America, I have never been more hopeful than I thought. We will get there. I promise you."

November 4, 2008 will be remembered in the history of America, perhaps the history of world as well. A person born to a Black immigrant got elected as the President of America, the superpower of the world.

Just like the slogan of Obama's campaign, "The change," America's political face has changed dramatically.

Even though Obama was the first Black President in American political history, in some people's opinion he was the best presidential candidate who happened to be 'Black.' It was notable that he never uttered a single word about his racial background at any time during his campaign speeches to win the votes from his race.

Even though many Blacks of the older generation, including Rev. Jesse Jackson and Rev. Al Sharpton, tried their luck in presidential elections in the past, they could not succeed. For millions of Americans Obama lifted the nation and, for most of the people, the 2008 election and Obama's victory was 'a dream come true.' A dream they never expected to live in their lifetime. In my viewpoint, he is also the son of a first-generation immigrant who became the President of the country.

America went on to elect a Black President, and it looked as though the civil rights movement led by Martin Luther King and other civil rights activists found its conclusion with this victory. But unfortunately, racial prejudice and discrimination continued, and stereotypical profiling stayed.

After Michelle Obama became the First Lady, she once visited a store for shopping. An older woman who did not recognize her thought she was a worker at the store and asked for some help. The First Lady gracefully helped the lady and dismissed the incident saying that someone just needed help, and it didn't matter if she was the First Lady or not.

President Obama also had his own share of racial profiling too. In his younger days, he was mistaken for a 'valet' and 'waiter' at parties he attended.

CHAPTER FOUR

In this country, it is very common that a person is evaluated and judged by their looks and skin color. To be considered as an American by Whites a person should have a white skin color. The stereotypical pre-assumption dictates the profession and education of a person, especially for immigrants. Even those born here to immigrant parents and are U.S. citizens by birth are not spared. As they have the same features as their parents except for one advantage— their ability to speak English without an accent. This helps them to overcome pre-judgment to some extent, especially on phone conversations.

There were many unfortunate incidents based on skin color and the race of people.

In 2018, two Black men were arrested from a famous café because some employees called the police and reported trespassing after they found the two were sitting out without ordering food. In fact, they were waiting for a friend to join them. People criticized the incident on social media saying that it happened because of their race.

In 1991, a Black man was charged and stopped by police for speeding his car on a freeway in Los Angeles. An argument erupted, and the police beat him physically.

A case was filed against the officers, but in 1992, these four officers were acquitted of the crime. When the verdict came, riots erupted in the Los Angeles area and continued for 5 days. Fifty people were dead and more than 2000 people were injured in the riots. It paralyzed Los Angles for more than 5 days, and protests erupted in defense of Blacks in several parts of the country.

In 2013, the "Black Lives Matter" movement began after the acquittal of the policeman in the shooting of a Black teenager and in 2014, after the death of two Black men in Ferguson, Missouri and in New York, 'BLM' became nationally recognized for street demonstrations.

Many incidents were reported where Blacks were shot and killed by police, and police officers were attacked in retaliation. Police departments all over the country were very concerned about the increasing friction between the public and police.

In the wake of all these shooting incidents, President Obama ordered that the police should wear 'body cameras' that record their interactions with civilians.

It is very unfortunate that all these incidents involving Blacks were happening while a Black person was country's President.

On May 25, 2020, a Black man was killed in Minneapolis, Minnesota while being arrested for allegedly using a counterfeit twenty-dollar bill in a store. During the arrest, a police officer knelt on his neck for a few minutes after he was already handcuffed and was lying face down on the pavement. Another Officer assisted him in restraining the man, while a third officer prevented bystanders from interfering. He had complained about being unable to breathe and continued saying, "I can't breathe." After several minutes he stopped speaking and lay motionless.

When the images of this incident, captured on the phone, and the CCTV cameras became public, it triggered protests all over the country and worldwide, sparking a debate against police brutality and racism.

Protestors in Minneapolis marched to the police precinct and broke the station windows and started fires around. A night-time curfew was imposed in Minneapolis and surrounding counties and national guards were deployed. The next day the Black Lives Matter movement took charge of the demonstrations. The protests gradually spread to over 2,000 cities in the country and also around the world. People called for reforms and defunding of police departments throughout the country.

The protests continued for several days. At least 200 cities-imposed curfews because of the unrest. Washington D.C. activated more than 60,000 National Guard personnel.

In Portland, protests took place for more than 70 days and Federal forces were deployed to subdue the protests.

'Wall of Moms', a movement organized by women against racial injustice, started by forming a 'wall' to protest in Colorado and became an instant 'icon of protest' across the country.

Within this time frame, shocking news came with a photo showing two police officers on horseback in Texas leading a Black man on a leash, a reminder of the way Blacks were treated in the slavery era.

Some of the hit movies and dramas were cancelled because of their racist content. It seemed George Floyd's death shook up the world on racism.

But within a couple of months, another incident followed where a Black was seriously injured in a police shooting in Kenosha, Wisconsin and was left paralyzed waist down. The officers who responded to a domestic violence incident, shot him eight times at his back leaving eight holes in his body, as he was trying to get into his car.

This incident again sparked protests in Kenosha and across the country. Jacob Blake's shooting came as the country grappled with the treatment of Blacks at the hands of law enforcement officials, as well as racism.

Black community leaders across the country expressed their disappointment about the systemic racism in the country as the police force with impunity routinely killed Blacks.

The White House almost went into a lockdown, as the protesters closed in on the White House and the country witnessed civil unrest. The President asked the military to standby for a quick deployment in case of more violence. He threatened if the protestors came close to breaking the White House fence, he would let the most vicious dogs attack them.

It was also reported that when the protesters gathered outside the White House, secret agents rushed the President to a bunker inside the White House which was designed for emergencies like terrorist attacks. But the President later rejected it as fake news.

The protesters were tear-gassed, and the President threatened to use military to regain control of the demonstrations.

To everyone's amusement, after a while, the President came out and walked to the church situated across the White House and posed in front of the church with a bible in his hand, as if it was a photo-op. His supporters hailed it as an act of courage, but the evangelical leaders of the congregation of the church criticized the president's action for using the church for political advantage. Later the military General who accompanied the President to the church felt he shouldn't have done that and looked down on this action.

The President deployed military personnel in Washington D.C. and other places where there were protests as he presented himself as a 'law and order President.'

This happened for the first time since the 1992 race riots in Los Angeles. The President also threatened to invoke the

'Insurrection Act of 1807' to mobilize the military in cities across the country to end the protests.

The deployment of the military was criticized by the former Defense Secretary as a 'Nazi tactic of dividing the people' instead of trying to unite people or at least pretend to try.

Activists called for reform and defunding police forces, but the President backed the police. He said that 'Law and order' is needed, not defunding and abolishing police.

Statues of Christopher Columbus and statutes of several confederate icons were being toppled across the country. 'Black Lives Matter' agitators demanded the removal of monuments, even those of country's Founding Fathers George Washington and Thomas Jefferson as they were also slave owners.

Within a few months after the Floyd and Blake incidents, another Black man was shot dead in Atlanta, Georgia after a scuffle with police officers while they were trying to handcuff him who was intoxicated.

The activists claimed the cops were employing lethal force against Black people at the slightest provocation. They are arrested or killed in large numbers across the country. I wonder why the police were not shooting below the knee or on the legs to detain and avoid shoot and kill.

In St. Louis, Missouri, a white couple stood outside their home pointing guns at "Black Lives Matter" protesters who were marching on the street close to their home. A video of this incident circled widely on social media and at the same time another video in which people shouted "white power" was circulated. The President proclaimed that there was nothing wrong with the white couple's actions as they were trying to protect their private property.

Another major protest erupted after a grand jury decided that none of the three police officers would be charged criminally for causing the death of Breonna Taylor, a Black woman who was an emergency medical technician (EMT). She was shot dead by officers dressed in plain clothes in a raid on her apartment located in Louisville, Kentucky, on March 13, 2020. The protesters chanted "All lives matter till Black Lives Matter."

BLM protesters clashed with Trump followers in Portland, and one person was killed in the clash. Portland had been the site of nightly protests for months since the killing of George Floyd.

The NBA decided to walk out of the games they were planning to protest over the shootings and killings of Black people in the country and they also encouraged other sports venues to follow their suit.

On April 20, 2021, the jury found the police officer guilty of murder in the death of George Floyd in 2020. He was found guilty of second and third degree murder and manslaughter. The other three officers are due to face trial later on for aiding and abetting charges.

Police brutality in the U.S looks like a never-ending story. On the same day, when the verdict in George Floyd's death was announced, a 15-year-old Black girl was shot and killed by police in Columbus, Ohio for holding a knife and trying to attack another woman.

Once, in a speech at a meeting, Martin Luther King said, "Protests and riots are the language of the unheard." He also said, "White America needs to understand that it has poisoned its soul by racism, and this understanding needs to be carefully documented and consequently is more difficult to reject. Blacks want social scientists to address the White community and tell it like it is – White America has an appalling lack of knowledge concerning the reality of Black life."

To understand and feel the pain of injustice a person faces, whether it is racial discrimination or anything else, one has to step into that person's shoes. Only those who have faced it, realize the impact. Most people suffer not because of their choice or fault.

The stains of hate in our country may take a long time to disappear and hopefully heal eventually.

CHAPTER FIVE

In 2010, America's deficit was 15 trillion dollars, the biggest since World War II. It was estimated that one out of eight citizens was living in poverty and on food stamps in that period. The unemployment rate was the highest in 45 years. These were the aftereffects of the 2003 Iraqi War which spent 800 billion dollars from the U.S. Treasury. In the war, 4500 American troops died and 3200 were injured. Also, 100,000 innocent Iraqi civilians died. Stocks plummeted down so bad, and it came as a blow to the otherwise bad economy. A decline in the middle-class and the large presence of poverty and hardness showed its ugly face in the richest country of the world.

In December 2011, President Obama declared the withdrawal of troops from Iraq. But many people thought the withdrawal would leave behind a destroyed, ruined and divided nation and so didn't get enough approval from the public.

In 2011, a movement called "Occupy Wall Street" was formed in Manhattan, New York by a group of people to protest the situation in the country. Zuccotti Park in Manhattan was occupied by the protesters. The protest was aimed at the wealthy people in the country, especially the Wall Street.

This was something never seen before in this country. The movement slowly started spreading across the country.

In the midterm poll of 2016, Democrats lost the majority. Republicans dominated both the houses. This came as a big blow to the Democrats.

In 2016, the next Presidential election campaign started, Hillary Clinton was chosen as the nominee for Democratic party. Even though there were other Democratic candidates, they could not get nominated.

In the meantime, Donald Trump started his campaign with a low profile and his ratings were very low initially, but he started getting support slowly from Whites, especially the jobless middle-class. His campaign slogans such as "Buy American," and "Make America Great Again" caught their attention and became a hit.

On the contrary, about 3 million people who didn't like Trump as a Presidential candidate signed a petition urging the electoral college to dump him from contesting. But nothing could stop him. Instead, surprisingly several other Republican candidates dropped out from the contest and ultimately Trump became the Republican nominee.

Trump emerged victorious in most of the states. This came as a shocker to his rivals and critics. Many people disliked his propaganda, especially people from Mexico, as he passed negative comments on them and also promised to build a wall at the border to stop them from coming to U.S. illegally. He also said that the illegal immigrants would be deported from the country, even though President Obama submitted a bill to stop deportation. But Donald Trump overcome all these obstacles, and won the election.

On November 8, 2016, Trump was declared to be the 45th President-elect. Vice-President-elect Mike Pence said to the people who gathered to congratulate the candidates, "This is a historic moment and American people have spoken."

After Mike Pence's speech, Donald Trump said, "We will make America great again!" Trump who had never held a position in government or in politics won the Presidency by a convincing campaign. He gained the support of the White middle-class, who felt they were left out in the American mainstream. His victory amounts to a stunning takeover of the Republican party by a candidate with no political experience. There were other Republican candidates who were more experience in politics and held higher governing positions, but they backed off from the campaign midway. There was no serious opposition left to block his path.

The Democratic party tried its best to denounce Trump with many negative remarks, including allegations of harassment toward women. But nothing could stop his destiny and he became the President.

Protests broke out across several cities following Trump's victory. Demonstrations gathered in front of Trump's properties in New York, Chicago, Washington and other cities. People held placards saying "Dump Trump" and "Not my President." Demonstrators included people from all ages, faiths and nationalities in 25 cities from New England to the Midwest. There were renewed calls to dispose of the electoral college system as Presidents are elected on the basis of electoral college majority despite getting lower popular votes than rival candidates. Trump got 46+% popular votes, less than the 48+% Hillary Clinton got.

Trump's strong showing in states, including Michigan, meant he won enough Electoral college votes to get elected as the President. Another example of the process is that in the 2000 election George Bush was elected President even though Al Gore won more popular votes than Bush.

Trump backers called the protesters 'crybabies,' asking them to accept the people's decision in a fair election. Trump's critics said that the protests were not so much about the results as against some of the xenophobic statements he had made. His statements to them were a matter of concern in a country that was becoming increasingly diverse, plural, multi-ethnic and engaged with the rest of the world.

On January 20, 2017, Donald Trump was sworn in as the President.

In his inaugural speech, he said, "A new vision will be born from today. The slogan is 'America First,' 'Buy American and hire Americans,' and we will protect jobs and manufacturing going out of the country and we will bring back our jobs by stopping the issuance and the abuse of H-1B visas where foreigners are hired for cheaper salary, thus not hiring Americans. People will be off welfare and back to their feet. We will eradicate terrorism from the face of the world. Together we will make America great again. Bring back our borders, bring back our jobs, bring back our wealth and bring back our dreams. Protectionism will lead to great prosperity and strength. America will start winning again like never before."

While Trump was delivering the inaugural speech, closer to the venue of the inauguration, a large group of protesters arrived with long wooden poles and bats and ran through the streets, slashed windows and clashed with police. The police responded with tear gas and stun-grenades to dissipate the protesters.

The next day after the presidential inauguration, protests started almost in all major cities. In Los Angeles, thousands of people who did not want Trump to be elected as president flocked on the freeways and stopped traffic.

Protestors also assembled in front of the Trump Tower in New York. In Oakland, protestors started vandalism and attacked police officers. About 2 million women marched in Washington to protest near White House. Several people were arrested, and the police used force and tear gas to disperse the protestors as they clashed with the police.

After the election, it seemed the country got fiercely divided into two sides. One side supported Trump and the other was anti-Trump. This divide became quite prominent in families and among friends. It turned people against each other in rural areas and across some of the most politically charged background states. There were instances of broken friendships, and neighbors turning against neighbors. In some schools, students started yelling at each other and with one group saying "build the wall" became a common sight.

In some households, people stopped talking to family members. Some said this was one of the crossroads crisis moments in the history. The election hardened an already clear racial divide in a former industrial city where 78% of the population was White and 18% were Black. Even husbands and wives argued and shouted in their relationship. Some blamed this divisiveness as a campaign rhetoric that inflamed racial, ethnic and class tensions that had simmered for long in the country. Angry and extremist language became a part of the mainstream. But Trump's triumph came with a silver lining. It demonstrated that the country was at a crossroads when change was inevitable, not just people.

After the election, during a speech Trump made for his supporters in Indiana, he warned that action would be taken on the companies who outsource manufacturing, as promised in the election campaign. He also warned that there would be 35% import duties of the products which were manufactured outside the U.S. and brought back.

Because of Trump's similar comments on this matter during the election campaign, not a single one of America's largest companies donated any money to his campaign. The chief executives of more than one thousand U.S. companies wrote an open letter to President-elect Trump. This letter said that American families and other communities could not truly prosper and reach their full potential in a country that was divided and distrustful.

On September 24, 2019, an independent inquiry was initiated by the House Speaker, and the House of Representatives. Trump was charged with abuse of power, for pressing Ukraine to assist in his 2020 campaign, damaging Democratic rivals and obstruction of Congress by accusing him of blocking testimony in response to House subpoenas.

Trump stated that the impeachment probe was a sham and a coup to nullify the result of the 2016 polls.

The House of Representatives voted to impeach President Trump on December 18, 2019 after several hours of debate. But the Senate had a Republican majority, and Trump was acquitted of the charges on February 5, 2020 after one and a half months' trial. Not a single Republican legislator voted against Trump.

On January 13, 2021 President Trump was impeached for the second time by the House of Representatives citing the riot and insurrection that occurred on January 6, 2021 at the Capitol Building.

The trial at the Senate for the second impeachment of Trump started on February 9, 2021. After several days, he left the office but was acquitted on February 13, with votes of 57-43 in which seven Republican Senators voted against Trump this time. Trump became the only President to be impeached twice by the House of Representatives in American history of 200 years and also acquitted both times by the Senate.

Out of three other Presidents who faced impeachment besides Andrew Jackson, Richard Nixon resigned before the trial and Bill Clinton was acquitted by the Senate and remained in Office.

CHAPTER SIX

After Bin Laden's death, everyone thought terrorism had almost diminished. But by 2013 another terrorist group by the name 'ISIS' was formed. They began their engagement in Syria and Iraq. Besides terrorizing people in those countries, they started giving warnings about their plans to attack the U.S. and its interests.

In 2017, the U.S. Government adopted strict security measures at several foreign airports where passengers boarded planes bound to the U.S. Laptops and cell phones with batteries inside were banned and could not be carried by the passengers. Also, the administration signed an order not to allow any more refugees to come to the U.S. from several Muslim countries and also restricted entry for those who even held immigration, visiting, or student visas. Immigration clearance became stricter at major airports.

People protested against the Administration's immigration policy across the country. Demonstrations were held at New York, Chicago, San Francisco and Los Angeles airports. On January 17, 2017, the Federal Appeals Court upheld a decision blocking those travel bans. It said, the Administration violated U.S. immigration law by discriminating against people based on their nationality, and it would hurt the American interests.

The Administration signed an order to build the wall at the Mexico border as President Trump promised in his campaign and also decided to deploy national guards at the Mexican border.

On February 16, 2017, "A day without immigrants," a protest in which restaurants, grocery stores, schools and several other establishments were shut across the country to protest against the Administration's immigration policies. People took part to show the importance of immigrants to the economy and also to protest against the racial profiling by immigration enforcement. But many people lost their jobs as employers were not in a mood to accept the movement.

A group of Indian students were sent back by the Homeland Security after they reached the U.S. on student visas to join a couple of colleges in Silicon Valley, California. Some of other students were not even allowed to board planes to the U.S. from a few airports where U.S. immigration officials were posted.

The Administration announced that immigrants would not get welfare in the first five years after they arrive in the country. They also decided to end DACA (Deferred Action ForChildhood Arrival), the program which granted working permits to those who arrived in the U.S. illegally as children and protected them from deportation. It seemed an end of the 'American Dream' for more than 8,00,000 young immigrants who entered the country as minors for no fault of theirs. The DACA program was supposed to allow a renewable two-years-permit to study and work in the country. This program was birthed by the 'Obama Administration', but it was one of Trump's campaign pledges to kill it.

Fifteen states and the District of Columbia sued to block the plan to end the program. Also, some of the giant tech companies pledged to stand by their employees against the Administration's decision. Ultimately, the Supreme Court ordered to keep the program until a final decision was made on the fate of the program.

In June 2017, in Los Angeles, protestors marched with signs saying "Impeach Trump" and stood near a mock casket. Impeachment protests across the nation clamored for the impeachment of the President.

On August 12, 2017, a "White Nationalist March" took place in Charlottesville, Virginia which included the Neo-Nazis, the Skinheads, and the KKK groups who carried sign boards that read, "Take America Back."

Another group was also present there, they carried placards that read "Black Lives Matter" and "Love" to protest against the "White Nationalist" rally.

A car suddenly rammed into the crowd and killed 3 people and left dozens injured.

Tens of thousands of demonstrators marched against the hate and the fatal violence that took place in Virginia. The demonstrators surged into the streets and parks across the country to denounce racism, white supremacy and Nazism.

On October 31, 2017 on "Halloween Day," a young man from the country Uzbekistan mowed down pedestrians and cyclists on the streets of Manhattan, New York by a pick-up truck. Eight people were killed and more than 11 people, including 2 school children, were injured seriously in the attack which happened just a few blocks away from 9/11 memorial 'Ground Zero'. The man was shot down by the police, and they found a note left at the spot by him claiming support to ISIS as he was radicalized by them.

Within a couple of months after this incident another person from Bangladesh detonated a pipe bomb strapped on his body in the 42nd Street passageway tunnel in Midtown Manhattan and injured himself and three others. Luckily, the bomb did not fully detonate, thus saving many lives. He told investigators that he did it in retaliation for U.S. air strikes on ISIS targets in Syria and Iraq.

After these incidents, the President urged to stop the immigration systems that allowed extended family members to get green cards and also the visa lottery system.

In January 2018, the Republicans proposed a crackdown on illegal immigrants and a sharp reduction in the number of illegal immigrants to the U.S. Immigration agents raided "7-Eleven" stores nationwide and arrested 21 people suspected of being in the country illegally and gave owners a tight deadline to prove that their other employees were authorized to work. The immigration office stated that the actions sent a strong message to those U.S. businesses who hire and employ an illegal workforce. The message was clear, if they were found to be violating the law, they would be held accountable. Notices of inspection were delivered to several 7-Eleven stores across 17 states. Also, the Administration decided to stop the spousal permit visas which allowed spouses of H-1B visa holders to work with new restrictions on H-1B visas issued to foreign workers.

In January, 2018, the President slapped steep tariffs on imports of washing machines and solar panels as part of the 'America First' approach. Over 95% of America's solar panels are imported from countries like South Korea, Malaysia, and China. The U.S. ran a bilateral trade deficit of 504 billion dollars with China, and the Administration decided to impose 60-billion-dollar tariffs on Chinese merchandise. China feared these American perfectionist measures.

China retaliated by enforcing huge tariffs on more than 100 products imported from the U.S., especially agricultural and meat items which did hurt the U.S. economy and put farmers in big trouble. Because of the trade wars between the U.S. and China, 'Wall Street' slumped, and stocks fell down drastically.

Subsequently, the Administration also declared to impose tariffs on all steel and aluminum imported from China and other countries citing a threat to national security as they could affect the validity of U.S. manufacturers who made planes and other military products. But the tariffs really affected small manufacturing companies including a leading nail factory which was forced to start laying off their workers due to loss. Also, a leading bike manufacturing company started planning to shift their production units out of the country because of the heavy tariffs on imported parts.

As the announcement of tariffs came out, warehouses throughout the country started heavily stockpiling inventory of all kinds of Chinese imports including microwaves, vacuum cleaners and filters, swimwear, furniture, etc. Also, retailers stocked up inventory to avoid higher tariffs before it kicked in.

CHAPTER SEVEN

I was able to read, write and speak English even before coming here as English was taught as the second language from the school level in my home country. I thought, I spoke fluently, but my presumption went in vain. People here perceived my way of speaking English with a foreign accent, not clear enough as per American standards. And people often expressed that they could not understand me well, and some people even laughed at the way, I pronounced certain words. But later, I realized the fact that American English also was spoken with several different dialects such as southern, northern, and even every other state had its own dialect. So, what was the big deal about my accent? I wondered. I used to get annoyed with the several "excuse me!" I received from people to repeat the words and sentences.

One time at an interview for a job, the interviewer could not understand some of the words I said. I lost my patience and asked the interviewer what is the reason for not following me even though, I spoke English well. To my surprise the interviewer said that I spoke English, but not with the right pronunciation and clarity to be understood. My confidence level which I had until then went down to an all-time low and everything around me seemed disastrous. After this incident, I became very self-conscious and hesitant to speak English every time I had to.

The funny thing is that within a few years after my arrival here, the people who could not understand my "accented English" were forced to follow the English spoken with foreign accents, especially the Indian accent as the customer care service calls of many major American companies were answered by the employees of the call centers which were outsourced to India and other countries. I could imagine the frustration of the people when they had to speak with those call center employees. But the people had no choice except to cope with the frustration of understanding the accents and get familiarized with the way they spoke as most of the customer service calls were transferred automatically to the call centers in a foreign country. I never ever imagined, one day the same people who could not understand my accented English would be forced to understand the same. What a strange turn of events!

Just like the customer service care was being outsourced, many branded products also got manufactured in countries such as China, Korea, Taiwan, Mexico, India, Pakistan, Bangladesh and so on. The reason was cheap labor and huge profit margins for the companies.

I would like to mention a funny, but real story here. Once, an Indian living in the U.S. went to India on vacation and purchased a shirt which he bought for his best friend as a gift. But when his friend opened the package, he was shocked to see the label on the shirt read, "Made in India" instead of "Made in America" as he expected!

It was not just the branded items, but other general consumer items were also being manufactured in other countries especially China. The chain stores named '99 Cents' have mushroomed in every corner of the country where many household products are sold for merely '99 cents' which was much cheaper than what people paid a few years back for the same kind of products which were made in U.S.

Because of the outsourcing trend thousands of American workers lost their jobs as many factories were forced to shut down, and many office workers lost their jobs as back-office support work was being outsourced to foreign countries.

These were the main reason for adopting Trump's election campaign slogans such as "Make in America", "Make America Great Again", which became popular and successful as many of Americans lost their jobs, income, homes which this led them to bankruptcy and poverty.

There were incidents when some products like toys manufactured in China had to be recalled in thousands because 'lead poison' was detected in the paint used on the toy. The authorities warned that it was unsafe for children. But surprisingly after a brief period, the toys were back on the racks hopefully after the corrections were made, and people did not hesitate to buy them because of the cheaper price.

Also, a lot of companies started hiring computer professionals such as 'software engineers' and 'computer programmers' from other countries as they were willing to work for a much lower salary than American professionals were paid.

People were brought on a job visa program called 'H-1B' citing the reason that there were not enough qualified Americans to fill the vacancies, but American workers claimed that this was not true, but was all about the lower pay. This practice led to a loss of jobs among hundreds of Americans who were replaced by H-1B visa holders. Adding insult to injury, American workers were asked to train those H-1B people before they left the company.

Some American workers at a major corporation filed a lawsuit against the company, and a foreign company who supplied the IT professionals. These American workers who were working for this corporation for more than 10 years were told one day that their jobs would end in 90 days and also that they would have new better jobs afterwards, but they would have to re-apply. Their jobs were turned over to the new workers who came from foreign countries through the contractors who provided workers, and the American workers were asked to train them also. They happily did, thinking that they would be offered new better jobs once these people were trained as promised. The lawsuit claimed that the companies broke the U.S. law by using H-1B visas to bring immigrant workers secretly and knowingly that the American workers would lose their jobs, and it was an abuse of H-1B visa program by American companies and their foreign recruiters.

According to a report, the immigrant workers were not even that skilled, but American workers trained them to be efficient. It was very stressful for the American workers to train those new workers because of many factors including language barrier and cultural differences. This came as an utter shock to more than 250 American workers, even though they trained the new workers in the hope of getting new good positions as they were promised, they were laid off instead. They lost their jobs and became broke within no time. Even though the laid off people applied for many other jobs within the company and even at other companies, they did not get any job. After the lawsuit against the corporation, it came to light that many other companies also did the same practice by hiring H-1B visa holders not only as computer professionals but also on positions in accounting, administration, etc.

Also, there were complaints filed with the Equal Employment Opportunity Commission (EEOC) by American workers against foreign owned companies and its foreign employees for discrimination. Previously, these kinds of complaints were usually filed with EEOC were by foreign immigrant workers who claimed to be discriminated by American firms and its employees. Now it is the other way around. What a change!

Another complaint filed by some American workers was that at an IT company based in U.S. where they were working, their foreign supervisors spoke in their native language with other foreign workers often in front of them which made them uncomfortable and left them feeling excluded from the official discussions at meetings.

An American who was the head of immigration at a major IT company filed a lawsuit against the company accusing it of discrimination. He alleged that the company preferred employees of South Asian race, especially Indian. He was terminated because he reported discriminatory treatment from senior officials of the company.

New York State fined a major IT company with one million dollars for visa violation. The settlement resolved that the company routinely brought foreign IT personnel into New York to perform work in violation of the terms of their visas and undercutting New York workers.

There were many lawsuits filed against foreign IT companies related to discrimination of U.S. origin employees.

Between 2016-18, H-1B usage was brought down to 43% because of localization. But by 2018, it was estimated that there was a shortage of roughly 2-5 million jobs to be filled in science, tech, engineering, math skills, and computer related work.

CHAPTER EIGHT

Back in my home country, I have witnessed how people, especially youngsters, were obsessed with the movie stars. The stars are treated like 'Gods' particularly if they have played mythological and religious characters. In some regions there are temples built in honor of some of the movie stars. There are 'fan clubs' for almost every leading star, and the fan clubs play an important role in helping the stars promote their films and make them successful.

There would be a massive celebration in front of the theaters on the day of the release of new movies of their favorite stars which would stun the people in America. The activity of the celebrations by the fans are beyond the imagination of American movie actors and the viewers.

It is that crazy in some of the regions that you would not believe your eyes. Inside the theaters, fan-club members of a particular star would clap and whistle whenever the hero of the movie appears on the screen, especially when he delivers a 'punch dialogue' or beats the villain. At the same time, the fan-club members of another rival actor would try to disturb the audience by 'boos' and inflict other disturbing damage to the movie's credibility. And many times, it would end up with verbal and physical fights between the two fan club members inside the theater and also outside – to save the image of their favorite actors.

The stars have a great influence on the people, on what they wear, eat, drink and all other products people use every day, through their commercials to promote different products. People follow the stars and copy their image.

Also, many stars would break into politics after they become popular and influential. Many of them form their own political parties and become leaders and ultimately hold higher positions in the government.

This may come as a shock to a normal person but there were incidents where some crazy fans immolated themselves when their favorite actors passed away.

I thought this kind of craziness existed only in my home country, but I was surprised to see that it existed here as well, but in a different way. Here people mostly are curious to know about the celebrity's personal life— what they wear, eat, what kind of cars they drive, the kind of exercises they do, where they shop, dine, whom they are dating, when are they getting married, getting pregnant, delivering, the kids' gender, separation, divorce and what not.

I found there are several 'tabloids' which publish exclusive features on celebrities' life and their activities that people are so curious to know and love to read. Now-a-days these stories are circulated more on social media networks. Also, I came to know about a special kind of reporters who are known as 'paparazzi.' They go around following and prying on celebrities and take their photos and videos, write stories and sell them to the media. As the media is willing to pay huge amounts of money for these pieces, the paparazzi are willing to take a lot of risk to get the materials, even if they were attacked sometimes physically by the celebrities or their bodyguards for invading their privacy.

Many times, the celebrities had to call the police but the paparazzi would flee the area before the police arrived and they would be back in business in no time. Even if the police find them, they are helpless in taking any action against them as there is no law prohibiting the paparazzi, and they also have the same rights like any other citizen who have the freedom to stand, to move around in public places unless they break any laws.

The celebrities even tried to enforce a law by writing to the government to prevent the harassment from the paparazzi, but till date no law has been passed and hence they continue their business as usual.

The lives of several celebrities have been disturbed because of the circulation of these stories, especially on social media. This kind of gossip news also existed in the past, but not to this extent because media coverage was not as much as it is now. Today, the news can reach millions of people around the world in seconds through electronic media.

Celebrities, in fact, have no privacy at all with their fame and money and they have no choice, but to suffer and pay the price of being a celebrity.

Another matter which surprised me is that a lot of people are crazy to buy items like dresses, costumes, and other personal items used by the celebrities which are sold at auctions by paying huge amounts of money!

Before coming here, I used to read news about divorces among some celebrities in newspapers once in a while, but I had no idea about the divorce rate among the general population. I later learned that the divorce rate is around 15%. According to studies, the adverse effects of divorce and trauma are more on the children as they are caught between the legal battle of the couple and custody battle of the children. However, kids love both the parents regardless of what the conflict is in their marriage.

Also, I learned that there are thousands of children living in broken families and foster homes due to divorce and with adopted parents because they were born out of wedlock to teenagers who couldn't afford to take care of them. It is an unfortunate fact that many children who live with adopted parents are not aware of who their biological parents are!

CHAPTER NINE

'Yoga' which originated in India has become so popular among people here especially with the celebrities. As the general population follows what celebrities do, 'yoga' and 'meditation' became an obsession among them as well. Yoga is supposed to be a spiritual form of exercise which is supposed to be non-commercial, but unfortunately it turned into a thriving business here promoted by the self-made yoga 'Gurus'.

Many people, including celebrities, go to India in search of happiness and peace of mind through yoga, meditation and spirituality. But on the contrary, the funny thing is that thousands of people from India wanted to come here chasing the 'American Dream' at any cost!

I also observed that several words like 'Karma', 'Guru', 'Pundit', 'Namaste', 'Avatar', 'Mogul', 'Kama Sutra' etc. from Indian vocabulary had become common usage among people here especially in the media.

At the time of my arrival, men and women used to mingle freely at working places, social gatherings, etc. than in my home country where people followed certain traditional restrictions on these situations. But that scenario has changed dramatically in the recent years. Now men have to think twice before they say something, gesture, extend hands to touch, hug or even handshake. They have to be very careful even how to say a compliment to a woman on her dress or looks as men are not sure how they would react to some of these actions could be interpreted as sexual harassment which are prohibited by the law.

In 2017, a feature story was published in a leading newspaper about a producer at a leading Hollywood movie production company. The story alleged sexual harassment by the producer of female actors. After that, several other established and famous actors came forward openly accusing him of sexual harassment and rape. Following this, a movement named "Me Too" formed, and several other men in the field of entertainment, politics and business were also exposed as such accounts of sexual harassment by a lot of women started to surface. Because of this movement, dozens of prominent men had to quit or got fired from high profile posts. These sexual harassment incidents were not limited just to female actors, but even a few male actors also came forward accusing some of the male actors.

The "Me Too" movement has dampened one traditional route to dating which is 'office romance,' and it was reported that there is a sharp decline in romance at offices now.

Across the business world, men adopted controversial strategies for the "Me Too" era. They did not want dinners with female colleagues any more, did not want even to sit next to them on flights or book rooms on the same floor when they had to travel officially together, and no more one-on-one meetings. A study among many senior executives found that many were spooked by the "Me Too" movement, and it was creating a sense of 'walking on egg shells.' They felt uneasy and fearful being alone with female colleagues as they were trying to protect themselves. Also, the study predicted if men avoid working or traveling with women alone for fear of being accused of sexual harassment the chances are the sexual harassment complaints might turn into sexual discrimination cases.

The "Me Too" movement became a sensation and very popular within a short time and was followed by thousands of women around the world.

Before coming here, I never had any idea about the gay and lesbian community as they were not active in the public openly at that time in my home country. Even here, for many years after my arrival they were living very secretively, hidden from the mainstream society because of the fear of being looked down upon, with prejudice, harassment and also physical attacks. But slowly they started coming into the public limelight identifying themselves and also formed a group named LGBT which is now known as LGBTQ. They started demanding the right to live in society without fear of discrimination and prejudice. They conduct rallies every year throughout the country to mark their movement, and the general population were stunned to see that thousands of them existed. Some of the states even legalized marriage among gays and lesbians.

I would like to mention a funny thing here. It is a common sight in my home country that the people from same gender who are straight often hold hands together or put hands on one each other's shoulders while moving around in public. Many American tourists often mistook them for gays and lesbians and thought my home country was much more advanced in this matter than America. They mentioned this to their relatives and friends who were surprised and delighted with dismay!

Reality shows are very common in the country now-a-days. There are several shows where one can show their talents like singing, dancing, comedy, acting, etc. But there are also shows about real legal cases which are taped and telecasted on TV. I was shocked to see the kind of cases presented on these shows. Friends, ex-husband, ex-wives, boyfriends, girlfriends, parents, children, in-laws are all suing each other for small amounts of money and even for silly matters. Also, there are paternity cases to prove the father-hood of the children filed by women.

I was wondering how could people be on such shows without any embarrassment which millions of people watched!

CHAPTER TEN

The U.S. is among the few countries where the right to possess firearms is conditionally granted by the 'Second Amendment' of the Constitution. About 30% Americans own guns, almost 390 million guns. This country has witnessed a pattern of mass shootings that has no parallel anywhere in the world. Around 150,000 people have already been killed in gun homicides within a span of 15 years.

In October 2017, an elderly retired man shot and killed 58 people and injured more than 500 people at a Las Vegas concert. He shot the people through a window of his room of the hotel where he was staying near the venue of the concert. It was assumed that he was planning the shooting for many days while staying at the hotel, and nobody noticed or suspected him even though he carried several guns in suitcases to his room on different days of his stay. Until now, nobody found out his real motive behind the shooting, and he had no prior criminal records at all.

The Las Vegas mass shooting had re-ignited an old political debate in the country over strict gun laws. Pro-gun lobbies like

NRA spend millions in political funding against strict control laws. It is in the face of violence that strict gun control policies succeeded in reducing gun violence. Even right after the Las Vegas shooting, there were four more mass shootings reported within a brief period.

On February 7, 2018, a teenager who was expelled from a school in Parkland, Florida entered the school with a semi-automatic rifle and began shooting at students he encountered in the hallways and on the grounds. He killed 14 students and three teachers. He had no criminal history, but his childhood was troubled, he had emotional problems including flashes of rage and was diagnosed with autism. He even posted a comment on social media quoting, "I am going to be a professional school shooter." But no one took it seriously and no investigation was conducted at that time. This teaches us a lesson that all threats should be taken seriously.

One of the students who survived the shooting ignited anger against gun supporting politicians while urging students to go political and teach such lawmakers a lesson. The student made an angry and fearful speech and urged students to register to vote as 4 million high school students would be eligible to vote by the mid-term elections in November 2018.

There were seven school shootings in 2018 itself and nearly 200, over the last 18 years.

From 2013-2018, there were more than 1800 shooting incidents and out of that around 2300 people died and 7000 were left wounded. There were more than 300 mass shootings in 2015, almost one shooting daily.

The Republican party held a majority in the House and many of its conservative lawmakers were funded by the NRA and other gun rights organizations which spent nearly 55 million dollars in the 2016 election despite so much gun violence.

Just four months after the horrible shooting incident at the school in Florida, a man entered a high school in Texas and opened fire and killed eight people and injured many. There were almost 22 shootings since the beginning of the year 2018.

All these incidents clearly indicate that mental illness is a leading problem among people in our country regardless of age, race or religion, and the easy availability of guns make it much worse.

President Obama stressed a gun control strategy, but many people, especially NRA members, were against it, saying that people have the right to own a gun to protect themselves from criminals. President Obama pleaded for strict gun control as the shooting incidents had become a routine time in the country. According to different surveys 70% of people think gun laws should be tightened.

The gun lobby led by the NRA spends millions of dollars every year to 'protect the Second Amendment', the right to bear arms, written in 1791 during the era of musketeers when the country's founding fathers felt such weapons were necessary for self-defense to resist oppression and for the security of a free state. The NRA defended their stand by saying that it was necessary to fix the broken mental health system, strengthen background checks to ensure records of people who are prohibited from possessing firearms, secure the schools and prevent mentally ill people's access to firearms.

The students who survived the shooting of the school in Florida marched to the White House demanding changes to U.S. gun laws calling out President and NRA. Also, students participated in anti-gun demonstrations all over the country.

Over 800 protests took place simultaneously across the country. They called for increased restrictions on sale of firearms and warned lawmakers that they would lose their votes if they didn't act. Hundreds of thousands of youngsters and their supporters chanted "Never again" and called for action and demanded to tighten gun laws. Young marchers filled streets in cities all over the country. "March for our lives" rallies had become common in the nation.

On March 24, 2018, more than 80,000 protestors turned up for protests in Washington D.C. which was the largest single day protest in the capitol. On March 14, 2018, Women's March organizers planned a national school walkout and marched to Washington D.C. and demanded the shutdown of NRA.

The youth vowed to continue their fight for their dead friends. Even though there were numerous other school shootings in the U.S. before, this was the first-time when students have been galvanized into action in the most visible way.

The President decided to tighten checks on gun buyers and also raise the age to 21 for buying guns. The President also suggested teachers to be armed with guns to protect students from shooters. But his solution to school shootings created a great outrage from teachers, parents, and gun control advocates. Teachers protested the idea of carrying weapons to classrooms to protect children. They pleaded for better resources like more counselors to deal with disturbed students instead of suggesting dangerous ideas. 'The National Teacher's Union' also rejected the idea of arming teachers. One teacher said, "the day teachers were asked to carry guns in the classroom would be my last day and I would leave my dream job of a teacher." The teacher further added, that the kids need to learn with books and not to be scared of guns in a classroom," the teacher said.

Several companies withdrew concessions to NRA members in support of gun control activists and also urged several media channels to stop streaming the NRA TV channel. Several major airlines also decided to cut ties with NRA.

But surprisingly, even in the wake of these shootings, most gun shops reported increased gun sales. This proved that a majority of people were moving towards guns rather than away!

On March 16, 2021, a young man killed 8 people and one person was injured in a series of mass shootings at a couple of massage parlors in Atlanta, Georgia. Six of them were of Asian origin and were employees in the parlors and two were customers of American origin.

At the time of the reporting the incident, it was not certain what the motive was behind the shooting, but hate toward Asian community could not be withheld as more than 3000 hate crimes were reported against them lately. It included physical assaults, verbal abuse, and harassment, etc. which escalated during the Covid-19 pandemic. Chinese individuals were targeted because the Corona virus was detected first in China, and people thought that they were the reason for the spreading of virus in the U.S. They were even called with names such as 'China Virus' and Kung Flu. It came to a point that they, especially the elderly, were afraid to leave their homes to go out even for a walk as they were being attacked, assaulted, and robbed. Several elderly people were mainly targeted, spat on, verbally abused and asked to go back to their home country.

Within a week after the shooting incident in Atlanta on March 22, another mass shooting occurred at a grocery store in Boulder, Colorado, killing 10 people including a police officer. It was another young man again and the motive remained unclear at that time, but later it was reported that he was taking revenge for the ridicules faced in his school days because of his religion and foreign sounding name. He also became paranoid and thought people were after him.

It is a warning for those people who enjoy making fun of other people due to their names, religion, ethnicity, accent, features, skin color, gender identity, etc. Some of the victims of this kind of bullying or ridicule keep the grudge to themselves, and one day it comes out and they might take it out on innocent people. Many incidents similar to the Boulder tragedy have occurred before as well.

After a few days of the two mass shootings, another shooting occurred in Orange, South California at an office building. Four people including a child were killed and another person injured critically. It was reported as a premeditated attack related to a business and personal relationship which existed between the suspect and all of the victims.

On April 16, 2021, an ex-employee of a warehouse in Indianapolis shot and killed 8 people out of which 4 were of Sikh descent including 3 women. The motive behind the killing is still unknown, as the gunman killed himself, except the fact that he was mentally unstable.

On April 27, 2021, another shooting took place at a rail yard in San Jose, California. The shooter who also was an employee of the transit killed nine of his co-workers. It was revealed later that this man had a mass collection of firearms and ammunition stocked at his home. Also, in this case the gunman killed himself.

Within a few days on June 1, 2021, 2 people died and more than 20 people were injured after a mass shootout outside a banquet hall in Miami, Florida.

Another shooting in Austin, Texas left 14 people injured. The shooting occurred after midnight near a popular nightlife destination.

It seems the mass shootings had become a serial event. During the last 5 years itself 200 innocent people were killed in different shooting incidents. Surprisingly, still there are many states which allow people to carry guns without a permit/license or background check whether concealed or openly.

CHAPTER ELEVEN

The U.S. is the home to the most immigrants in the world. Fifty-nine million people have migrated since 1965 and at present has the world's largest immigrant population. Twenty-six percent of the population consist of immigrants and their U.S. born children. As more and more immigrants settle, more foreign languages spoken are heard and traditional dresses from different countries are worn, especially by women.

According to a study, it is estimated that by 2055 immigrants, especially Asians, would play an important role in shaping the future of this country.

A body builder from Austria who came here to pursue his body building career became a famous movie star and subsequently got elected as the Governor of California, not once but twice.

People born from Indian immigrant parents became Vice-President, governors, surgeon general, and attorneys. These are among some of the prominent achievements of immigrants' children.

Studies revealed that of the American population in 1950 Whites were 85%, Blacks were 10% and Hispanic was 2%. By 2010, only 63% were white, but 16% were Hispanic and 12% were Black. Between 1998 and 2016 Hispanic geography grew dramatically and along with interracial marriages one may wonder whether the country is slowly turning into 'Brownish'. The U.S. is the second largest Spanish speaking country in the world as more than 52 million, one in every sixth person, speaks Spanish! Mid-western towns a couple of decades ago were 100% white, they have seen the Hispanic score a sizable majority between 2001-2016.

In 1994, white Christians made up 75% and by 2016 white Christians shrunk to 55%. Millions of Whites are anxious about their slide into minority status. Racial anxiety is deep in white American ethnicity. In 80's, nearly half of U.S. cities were 98% white, but today less than 5% are and turning into a minority.

In 2018, to enforce the Administration's Zero tolerance policy on illegal immigrants, as many as 2000 children were separated from their parents who were arrested after illegally crossing into the country. The children were held in erected tent structures near the border and also at military bases and detention centers at New Mexico. The U.S. military has been asked to build temporary tent cities to house illegal immigrants. It is estimated there were more than one million immigrants, including 20,000 children, stationed so far. Most of the people entered with an intention to unite with families who were already in the country or fleeing violence and prosecution in their home countries.

The civil rights activists have decided to file a lawsuit in the U.S. district court in California, citing violation of human rights. There were protests in California over the Administration's action of its 'Zero tolerance' border scrutiny policy. Because of the elevation of anger and protest all over the country, the Administration was pressured to reverse the order on family separation temporarily.

The policies reached new levels of toxicity and bitterness with social boycotting people from the administration. The White House Press Secretary was refused service at a restaurant in Washington. Also the Homeland Secretary was heckled at another restaurant.

The organizations that did the heckling said it was a part of protesting against Administration officials over its immigration policy which was cruel and animus.

The country was torn apart on the immigration policy. Along with the social boycott of White House aides, a White House advisor of the immigration policies and another supporter of the immigration policies were heckled and intimidated during their social outings.

In the middle of all these controversial incidents, the U.S. Supreme Court upheld the travel ban which was executed by the Department of Immigration to ban people coming to the U.S. from some of the Muslim countries. The court said that the President has the authority to ban travelers from certain countries if the President thought it was necessary to protect the country.

In the meantime, on the lawsuit filed by 17 Democratic leading states and ACLU, a U.S. District Judge in San Diego ordered that immigrant children and parents who were forcibly separated at the Mexican border be united within 30 days, and youngsters under 5 years be united within 14 days. The judge also issued a nationwide injunction against further family separations and ordered the government to provide phone contact between the parents and their children within 10 days.

On June 30, 2018, under the banner "Families Belong Together," more than 700 marches were held by thousands of people across the country to protest against the Administration's latest immigration policies. Parents and liberal activists who participated in the march said that they felt compelled to show up after heart-wrenching accounts of children forcibly taken away from their parents.

This was the first time Americans showed this kind of support for immigrants. The rallies got funded and supported by several leading social activist organizations.

About 30,000 marchers gathered across from the White House. The marchers expressed their feelings that the Administration's policy was barbaric and inhumane. Several Hollywood celebrities also joined the "Families Belong Together" march to protest against the Administration's immigration policies.

The President threatened to seal the U.S.-Mexico border entirely if the Congress did not approve the funding for the wall which was proposed and also change the immigration laws. The President also threatened to declare an emergency to get money for the border wall if Congress did not approve the fund.

The Administration deployed officers to arrest unauthorized immigrants in several cities, including Los Angeles, Chicago, New York in a move to battle against sanctuary policies which protect them from deportation and also proposed to scrap the H-1B lottery system and replace that with a 'wage based' selection process.

In July 2020, Immigration and Customs Enforcement ordered that all foreign students would be forced to leave the country or transfer to another college if their universities offered online classes only by the forthcoming semester.

Another order enforced suspension of green card and visas for a range of foreign guest workers. Thousands of foreign professionals found their future upturned, as in some cases families would be separated.

Also, the Administration decided to end the constitutional right to citizenship for the children born in the U.S. to non-citizens, un-documented immigrants and the visitors. There are about 3.8 million undocumented immigrants in the U.S. till date, who have at least one child born here.

Fearing a decision ending the right to citizenship, a record number of children born to non-citizens and un-documented immigrants started migrating to Canada seeking asylum.

On the contrary to this, close to the 2018 midterm election, two caravans of approximately 7000 migrants from countries like Honduras, Guatemala and El-Salvador who were fleeing because of violence, corruption and poverty came to the U.S. border in order to seek asylum.

The President criticized the 'caravan' as an invasion by the migrants and the Administration decided to deploy more than 5000 troops at the border with Mexico in order to stop the caravan and defend the border in case there was any kind of violence. There were already 2000 national guards deployed at the border.

Migrants are entitled under U.S. and International Law to apply for asylum. But the Administration invoked extraordinary national security powers to deny asylum to those migrants who entered the country illegally and described it as an invasion of the country.

Huge barricades and walls of barbed wire were erected on both sides of the U.S.-Mexico border near California to stop the caravan. Within a few days, the migrants tried to cross the border, and customs and patrol officers used teargas and rubber bullets to stop them and the migrants, which included women and children, had to run for life. After this incident, the President warned that the border would permanently be closed if necessary.

A new policy was introduced by the U.S. citizenship and immigration services on international students to bar re-entry for up to 10 years if they tried to work without authorization after leaving their studies, which violates the terms of their visa. Ten million foreign students were studying in the country to date. A person who overstayed more than 180 days before they departed from the country could be barred from re-entering for 3 years, and if it was more than a year, the barring would be for 10 years.

Democrats decided to raise their voice against this policy. A group of 18 Democrat senators wrote a letter to the director of the USCIS (United States Citizenship and Immigration Services) and asked to get rid of the unfair policy. International applications to US colleges dropped sharply due to the anti-immigrant policies.

A federal judge issued a restraining order, in the meantime, which temporarily halted the Administration's order denying asylum to the people who came in the caravan.

The naturalized citizens started getting worried as many were under the radar of Immigration Services because of differences in name, spelling, date and place of birth, etc. Because of this action, an Indian who was a naturalized citizen was already de-naturalized and deported. Also, there were cases of denying renewal of U.S. passports for thousands of people who were born to immigrants in the U.S. on the grounds of suspicion that the birth certificates could be obtained fraudulently.

CHAPTER TWELVE

The midterm election of 2018 took place on November 6. Just like the time of the presidential election in 2016, families in the country were sharply divided due to the recent political differences and developments. This mid-term election was the most important election in generations. America was at a crossroad. One hundred thirteen million people voted. Young people, and suburban voters, including more educated women, preferred Democrats and white rural men preferred Republicans. When the results came, Democrats took control of the House of Representatives, but Republications still kept the Senate.

Record numbers of women were elected to the House of Representatives. Forty-three women including Blacks, Latinos, Native Americans and Muslims made the most racially and ethnically diverse Congress House. Democrats won the Arizona Senate after a long period of 30 years.

Two weeks before the mid-term election about 13 bombs were sent to several high-profile Democrats and a famous actor who was a major critic of the current administration. Fortunately, none of the bombs exploded as they were detected as suspicious packages at the mail facilities before the delivery, so this avoided any casualties.

When the President nominated a judge who was accused of sexual harassment by one of his former high schoolmates, it became a national controversy. Women protested against his nomination throughout the country. At the same time a lot of men, especially white, started showing support for his nomination, and it became a fight between white men and liberated educated women. But in the end, the protests were in vain, and he was confirmed Judge to the Supreme Court after winning the majority votes in the Senate.

In December 2018, close to the Christmas holidays, the government shut down for the third time during the year. The reason for this shut down entailed the funds of 5 billion dollars meant for the construction of a wall at the U.S. border with Mexico as Democrats opposed the proposal.

Because of the government shutdown, thousands of federal employees and contract workers across the country panicked as they would not be able to receive their paychecks during the Christmas holidays. The President warned that the shutdown might be prolonged until he got his fund to build the wall.

The largest previous shut down was in December 1995, which lasted for 21 days and about 8 million federal employees and others were affected during the Christmas holidays.

The shutdown affected the government departments, including Transportation, Justice, Homeland Security, Housing, Agriculture, Commerce and the Treasury. Federal workers were temporarily laid off or worked without pay. Native Americans who receive federal funding struggled. National parks became hazardous without staff.

As the government shut down reached 22 days by January 12, 2019, it broke the previous record of the 21 days between December 1995 and January 1996.

Because Democrats didn't budge to the demand for the funding of the wall, the President threatened to declare a national emergency and build the wall using disaster relief funds and with the help of the Army Corps of Engineers.

It was reported that between 2005 and 2015, 4.4 million workers were laid off from Fortune 500 companies. At the age 50, 75% of people in the country were left with only 5000 dollars in their savings bank account. After the age of 65, 45% depended on relatives, 30% on charities, and 23% continued working because they could not afford to retire and work until they died. There are currently 40 million people in poverty and 34 million with no health insurance. 75% seniors cannot afford hearing aids and 65% do not have dental insurance. Half of the population lives paycheck to paycheck. More than 2,000 children are born as the result of rapes every year and more than 40,000 homeless adults sleep in shelters every night in major cities. In 2020, the U.S. national debt was around 23 trillion dollars.

America is still a great financial superpower as before. It survived more than 20 recessions and a great depression since 1990. But in 2015, program for International Students Assessment (PISA) showed that Americans were at the 38th position in science when compared with those in 71 countries. It is so unbelievable but regretfully worth mentioning that as per a poll conducted, many people in this country could not identify the U.S. on a world map!

Today American neighbors are more segregated than they were in the years immediately following the Civil War. As Martin Luther King said, "People fail to get along because they fear each other; they fear each other because they don't know each other; they don't know each other because they have not communicated with each other."

CHAPTER THIRTEEN

In Early 2020, an invisible virus named Covid-19 put the whole world's normal life into a standstill and brought human beings on their knees which made them helpless, scared and fearful for life. This pandemic changed the world, so as America.

By the end of 2019, the outbreak of this viral illness in Central China spread more widely across the nation sickening several hundred that crossed borders to five countries, including the U.S. Six deaths were reported after the new virus was detected in December 2019 in China's Wuhan province and the number of infections rose from more than 100 to 300 within a week. While the vast majority of the cases were in Wuhan, infections spread to other cities like Beijing Shanghai, Tunjin and Huan.

The U.S. set up airport check points in New York, LA, Chicago, Atlanta and San Francisco for passengers arriving from China.

Chinese authorities moved to lockdown in five cities with a population of millions. Within 3 months more people were infected outside China.

By March 2020 more than 4,000 people were infected and 69 were dead in U.S. The President planned to declare an emergency and shut down states which were hot spots as experts warned that up to 150 million people could be infected.

By April 2020, the U.S. had more than 324,000 infected cases and more than 9,000 deaths and the country moved to the top where Corona virus cases were more than any other, including China, Italy and Spain.

The country faced the worst jobless rate since the Great Depression as more than 16 million people sought unemployment aid in this period.

New York and California went into lockdown. New York City that never slept seemed to be fully asleep. New York was more affected as more than 12,000 people died and more than 4 million people were infected. The state slowly went into lockdown as it became one of the world's biggest hot spots. Nursing homes were affected badly.

By the end of April, there were more than 45,000 deaths in the country which was the world's highest and more than 815,000 people were infected. Most of the airports in the country were shut down. Nationwide, 8 million Federal employees were without any paycheck. Twenty-eight million people became uninsured.

Healthcare workers became scared of their life as a uniformed nurse was shot at in Oklahoma City. Some stupid people thought that health care workers were a cause of the spread of the virus rather than the saviors. Health care workers were advised not to go out in their uniforms or badges. It was very unfortunate that while they were putting their lives at risk to save others, they became the targets of hate!

In the meantime, people protested in front of the Michigan Governor's office for the order to be in lockdown because of the spread of the virus. They brought their cars on the roads and created a gridlock.

Also, in Minnesota protestors gathered outside of the Governor's residence demanding to lift the lockdown.

The country was divided over the lockdown. Some protestors were carrying posters saying, "Land of the Free," "The Infectious Disease Expert Lied," etc. The Protestors wanted to re-open the country for work to save their jobs, but they were not wearing masks, let alone social distancing which was supposed to save their lives! There were counter-protesters also who supported the lockdown, and they were carrying posters saying, "Safety First."

As the unemployment claims surged to over 30 million, the country was frustrated, anxious, scared, angry and faced the greatest challenge since World War II. All jobs created since the great recession were wiped out.

By the end of November 2020, a second wave of Covid-19 erupted, and cases topped 4 million. More than 170,00 people were tested positive on an average day as millions of people traveled for the long "Thanksgiving" weekend. Now the country's overall total from the pandemic became more than 13 million infections, the world's largest outbreak.

By the end of December, cases surpassed 15 million averaging more than 2,000 deaths a day.

The Center for Disease Control (CDC) urged people to postpone travel plans and stay home for the Christmas and New Year holiday season as the winter months would be the most rough and difficult time.

At the same time, the White House hosted Christmas parties with hundreds of guests, mostly without masks or social distancing as people believed the pandemic was either a hoax or its effect were exaggerated, and some didn't care and acted 'macho'.

On December 11, 2020, the FDA approved a Covid-19 vaccine for emergency use and planned to start vaccination as soon as possible. It was a huge relief as more than 3 million lives were lost by then, more deaths than in any other country and the infections still surged daily.

On December 14, the vaccine rollout began in all 50 states and planned to immunize 100 million people by March 2021 with priority for high-risk workers.

The Covid-19 pandemic gave a massive blow to already struggling retail stores in the country with massive debt and were facing bankruptcies and closure due to the shift in shopping habits. Over 8400 stores were shut down in the year 2020. The U.S. Government left with the biggest deficit since World War II. As per the Department of Commerce data contracted at a 48% annualized rate in January-March period in six years and the largest since 2008.

After wrecking havoc throughout 2020, the pandemic entered 2021 with no sign of slowing down. The U.S. recorded 20 million cases since the start of the pandemic, and the country added more than 2 million cases by December 2020. The country now accounts for nearly a quarter of the more than 83 million cases reported in the world and nearly a fifth of the death toll as it recorded for more than 3 million deaths so far. California became the new epicenter of the pandemic in the country.

To add fuel to the fire, a new variant of the virus was detected in UK and new infectious had more than doubled in recent weeks, because of the new variant. Drug makers rushed to test if the vaccines were going to stop the new virus variant.

Within a few days, the new virus variant was detected in US also. In Colorado, one person was infected with the new virus variant.

As of January 19, 2021, the death toll reached more than 4 million and by the end of February, the toll reached more than 5 million and still surged. More Americans have died from Covid-19 than they did on the battlefields of two world wars and the Vietnam War combined with more lives lost to this virus than any other nation.

On February 23, 2021, President Biden said in a solemn ceremony at the White House:

"Today we make a truly grim, heartbreaking milestone–500,071 dead," and he urged the nation to resist becoming numb to sorrow!

CHAPTER FOURTEEN

On January 6, 2021, a mob of supporters of President Trump attempted to overturn his defeat in the 2020 Presidential election. The riot led to the evacuation and lockdown of the Capitol. Five people died and dozens were injured including police officers.

On January 5 and 6, thousands of Trump's supporters assembled in Washington D.C. to support his claim that the 2020 election was stolen from him and also demanded that the Vice-President and the Congress reject Biden's victory. The supporters walked to the capitol building where a joint session of Congress was to begin counting Electoral college votes to certify Biden's victory.

The rioters breached police perimeters and stormed the building. They occupied, vandalized, looted the building for several hours. Police Officers and reporters were assaulted and attempts were made to take the lawmakers as hostage.

They chanted "Hang Mike Pence" before setting up gallows and noose outside, and they blamed him for not rejecting

Electoral College votes. They ransacked the House Speaker's office and also those of other members of the Congress.

Capitol police evacuated Senate and House of Representatives chambers and other buildings in the complex were also locked down. The Capitol was cleared of rioters by evening. The counting of the electoral votes resumed and was completed by early morning of January 7 and Vice-President Pence declared President-elect Biden and Vice-President-elect Kamala Harris.

Insurrections were not new to America and this one resembled what happened when Abraham Lincoln was elected in 1861 and also Rutherford Hayes in 1877.

The Capitol was locked down again on April 2, 2021 because a man rammed his car into a barricade outside the Capitol and killed one police officer. It was reported later that the suspect was a follower of the "Nation of Islam," a social movement of Blacks. Streets surrounding the Capitol and Congressional office buildings were locked down immediately.

On January 20, 2021, the country woke up from a bad dream. Around 11:30 A.M. the Presidential inauguration started. Around 25,000 National Guards were deployed in and around Washington D.C. Normally there would be millions of people assembled at the Capitol premises for the Presidential inaugurations, but due to the tight security after the January 6th siege, only selected guests were present.

Lady Gaga sang the National Anthem. Vice-President-elect Kamala Harris took the oath. This was another historic moment in recent years, especially because the first woman Vice-President in American political history was sworn in.

Jennifer Lopez performed the song "This Land is Your Land." Amanda Gorman, a young poet, recited her poem "The Hill We Climb" which delivered the message of unity. Garth Brooks performed "Amazing Grace."

After taking the oath as the 46th President, Joe Biden said in his inaugural speech, "Democracy won and I will be the President for all Americans."

Biden continued, "Democracy has prevailed in a country reeled amid and a violent melee two weeks ago at the U.S. Capitol. On this day, my soul is in bringing America together, uniting our people, uniting our nation and I ask every American to join me in this case. Uniting to fight anger, resentment, hatred, extremism, lawlessness, violence, disease, joblessness and hopelessness we face. With unity we can do great things. We can right the wrongs. We can deliver racial injustice and we can make America once again the leading force for good in this world. We can see each other not as adversaries but as neighbors. We can treat each other with dignity and respect. Without unity, there is no peace, only bitterness and fury. No progress, only exhausting outrage.

He then added, "Here we stand where 108 years ago at another inaugural, thousands of protesters tried to block brave women marching for the right to vote. And today we marked the swearing of the first woman in American history elected to national office, Vice-President Kamala Harris. Don't tell me things can't change."

Biden concluded, "I pledge this to you. I will be a President of all Americans. We must end this uncivil war."

Vice-President Kamala Harris said in her speech, "In many ways this moment embodies our character as a nation. It demonstrates who we are even in dark times. We not only see what has been, we see what can be. A great experiment takes great determination. The will to do the work and then the wisdom to keep refining, keep tinkering, keep perfecting. The same determination is being realized in America today. I see it in the scientists who are transforming the future. I see it in the parents who are nurturing generations to come and in the innovators, the educators, in everyone who is building a better life for themselves, their families and their communities."

While the preparations for the inaugural function was going on at the Capitol, Trump left for Florida after attending a meeting at 'Joint Base Andrews." In a brief speech he made at the meeting, he mentioned "we will be back in some form."

He decided not to attend the Presidential inauguration nor welcome the President and the First Lady at the White House as per the custom. He was the first President in more than 150 years to snub the inauguration of the successor.

The 2020 Presidential election was an epic and historic one. More people voted in this election than in any year since 1900. Prior to November 3 Election Day, 100 million people voted. In 2016 it was only 1.4 million by this time.

Also, this election was the most important one than any other in the American history. It was also one of the most controversial elections as a large number of people preferred mail-in ballots because of the Covid-19 induced pandemic and that led to the allegations of fraud and stealing of votes by Trump and his supporters. This election could shape the world like never before with the dirtiest poll battle in American history.

More than thousand candidates filed with the Federal Election Commission to run for President. There were nine women democratic candidates filed. Several Republican candidates filed, but the final candidate for Republican party was none other than Donald Trump. Joe Biden was picked as the candidate for the Democratic party.

Biden picked Kamala Harris as his running mate as the Vice-President. Kama Harris started as a presidential candidate and took part in the debate at the primaries and even had an argument on a sensitive topic with Biden. She had to drop out later due to the lack of funds for her campaign.

Trump tried to portray Kamala Harris as ineligible as she was born to immigrants and described as an 'anchor baby' as her parents were non-citizens at the time of her birth. Kamala Harris was born from a Black father and an Indian mother who were both immigrants. Trump made the same accusation about President Obama at the time of his candidacy, accusing that he was not born in the U.S.

On September 30, the first debate between Biden and Trump took place. Unfortunately, the debate was dubbed by the media as '90 minutes of chaos.' There were interruptions and insults. Trump interrupted Biden around 75 times. One time Biden was even forced to tell Trump to "shut up."

When Trump was asked about supremacist organizations, he hesitated to condemn. Trump warned if the election was not going to end well and if he loses, there wouldn't be a peaceful transfer of power. He insisted that he would not accept the results of the election if it went against him.

For several polls, people opinioned that this was the worst Presidential debate they have ever seen.

About 81 Nobel Laureates endorsed Biden for the Presidency. They cited Biden's willingness to listen to experts and his deep appreciation for using science. But Trump called Biden "a low energy and sleepy Joe," and said a 'weak' Biden would destroy the 'American Dream.' He asked whether the country could save the 'American dream' or would be allowed a socialist agenda to demolish it. Also, he accused Biden and Kamala Harris as being responsible for the race unrest which took place in the country by the 'Black Lives Matter' movement. He said most of the protestors were anarchists and criminals who threatened citizens and their property through looting, and it would be dangerous to the country.

Biden shot back and said Trump was the one who rooted violence so that he could blame the Democratic party and with the election on that shield against the 'stolen election.'

On November 3rd, Election Day, Joe Biden was leading with 214 electoral votes and by November 6th he was leading by 253 and on November 7th Biden surpassed 270 and got 306 electoral votes which validated Biden's winning. Trump tweeted that he won the election by a lot even though he got only 232 votes.

Biden won back the battleground states of Michigan, Wisconsin and Pennsylvania, the states that delivered the presidency for Trump in 2016.

Biden and Harris won 75 million popular votes, 4 million more than Trump, a victory more than any ticket in U.S. history.

Trump was not willing to concede the defeat, and he claimed victory himself. He said he would move to the courts for re-counting as he pointed out that mail-in votes were not legal and a fraud.

Protests by Trump supporters started across the country with slogans like "stop counting." Protesters marched through the streets of several cities in response to Trump's aggravating effort to challenge the vote count. In Phoenix, Trump supporters, some of them armed, gathered outside the 'county' recorder's office where a closely watched count of votes was being conducted.

Another group of pro-Trump 'poll watchers' gathered outside a ballot counting center in Detroit, demanding to 'stop the count." Also, counter-protests with slogans such as "count every vote" marched through Washington D.C., just a block away from the White House.

Trump claimed that he had won the election long before key states had counted all the ballots. He spent much of his days asserting that people were trying to 'steal' the election from him and cast doubt on the legitimacy of the mail-in votes.

Dozens of armed protesters descended on the residence of Michigan Secretary of State in the night using megaphones, shouting obscenities, threatening and chanting into bull horns to intimidate the Secretary and the family. The crowd was made up of people angry over Trump's election loss. They shouted and chanted slogans echoing conspiracy theories about the election process, and they wanted to overturn the election results.

The country seems to be divided perhaps into Red and Blue like never before.

After the Supreme Court rejected the lawsuit by Trump and his lawyers, thousands of his supporters marched in Washington D.C. and several state capitals to protest the stolen election.

There were confrontations between protesters and counter-protesters which escalated into violence. In Washington D.C. four people were stabbed and one person was shot. Signboards of "Black Lives Matter" which were erected on some churches were pulled down and burnt.

In his speech after the victory, Biden pledged that he would seek to unify the country. He said, "The people of this nation have spoken. They have delivered us a clear victory. I am humbled by the trust and confidence you have placed in me. I pledge to be a President who seeks not to divide, but to unify. To make progress we must stop treating our opponents as our enemy. We are Americans. We must restore the soul of America and end an era of demonization!

Also, Biden promised Kamala Harris that she would have the same access to the Oval office that he did as Vice-President and would be the last one to offer advice after a meeting.

Kamala Harris said in her speech, "We the People have the power to build better future, protecting our democracy. It takes sacrifice, but there is joy in it. We, the people, have the power to build a better future. While I may be the first woman in this, I won't be the last. Because every little girl watching tonight sees that this is a country of possibilities. And to the children of our country regardless of your gender, our country has sent you a clear message. Dream with ambition, lead with conviction and see yourself in a way that others might not see you, simply because they have never seen it before."

Also, she said that she was thinking about her mother and about the generations of women - women who fought and sacrificed so much for equality, liberty and justice for all, including

Black women who are too often overlooked, but so often provided that they are the backbone of our democracy.

She concluded, "To the American people, no matter who you voted for, I will strive to be the Vice-President that Joe was to President Obama— loyal, honest and prepared, waking up every day, thinking of you and your families because now is when the real work begins. We have elected a president who represents the best in U.S. A leader, the world will respect, and our children can look up to a President for all Americans."

Barack Obama mentioned in a speech about how his mother's teachings influenced and guided him through his Presidency. He quoted his mother's advice as, "Be kind and be useful and caring about people who are less fortunate than you. Be a peacemaker rather than an instigator. Try to lift people up instead of putting them down."

"The U.S. President is the most powerful person on earth. What that person does changes life for all of us. There are consequences to a President's actions. It affects how the world looks at America. The behavior matters, character matters."

President Biden inherited nothing when it came to a plan for vaccination by the previous administration. But the President planned and executed the order to start vaccinating people as soon as possible with a target of 100 million doses in 100 days.

As more than 100,000 Covid-19 cases were reported over the past month, almost every day and was still surging, the President signed an order mandating masks to be worn in the federal buildings and requested people to wear masks on all the interstate travels, including planes, trains, ferries, buses and other public transportation.

Also, President Biden signed orders including reversal of tough measures on immigration such as DACA and also travel restrictions from several Muslim and African countries and to halt the construction of the border wall with Mexico. Also, he signed a letter to re-enter U.S. in the 'Paris Climate-Agreement'. The Administration decided to bring back all the troops back from Afghanistan by August 31st, 2021 after nearly 20 years, ending the longest war in American history.

America keeps on changing and who knows what would be the next big surprise stored in the near future?

AUTHOR BIO

KevyArgy is the pen name of the author. He has published articles, short stories in periodicals, and a collection of short stories in a language other than English. *A Changed America* is his first book in English. He is also an actor. He migrated to the US in 1986 and lives in New York.